★★★★★

MLB TEAMS

Washington NATIONALS

KENNY ABDO

Fly!
An Imprint of Abdo Zoom
abdobooks.com

abdobooks.com

Published by Abdo Zoom, a division of ABDO, P.O. Box 398166, Minneapolis, Minnesota 55439.

Printed in the United States of America, North Mankato, Minnesota.
102025
012026

Photo Credits: AP Images, Getty Images, Shutterstock
Production Contributors: Kenny Abdo, Jennie Forsberg, Grace Hansen
Design Contributors: Candice Keimig, Neil Klinepier

Library of Congress Control Number: 2025936808

Publisher's Cataloging-in-Publication Data

Names: Abdo, Kenny, author.
Title: Washington Nationals / by Kenny Abdo
Description: Minneapolis, Minnesota : Abdo Zoom, 2026 | Series: MLB teams | Includes online resources and index.
Identifiers: ISBN 9798384940371 (lib. bdg.) | ISBN 9798384941132 (ebook) | ISBN 9798384941514 (read-to-me ebook)
Subjects: LCSH: Washington Nationals (Baseball team)--Juvenile literature. | Baseball teams--Juvenile literature. | Professional sports--Juvenile literature. | Sports franchises--Juvenile literature. | Major League Baseball (Organization)--Juvenile literature.
Classification: DDC 796.357--dc23

Table of CONTENTS

NATIONALS

In the heart of the nation's capital, the Nationals bring baseball pride to Washington, DC. With power at the plate and strength on the mound, this team keeps America's pastime alive!

ABRAMS
5

As one of Major League Baseball's (MLB) newest teams, the Nationals have made a big impact in a short time. From thrilling comebacks to championship moments, they proudly represent the red, white, and blue.

SHOW SOME
NATITUDE
NATIONALS
NATIONALS PARK
The Washington Post
PNC
Budweiser
Coca-Cola
BETMGM
GEICO
VENTURE GLOBAL

BATTER UP!

Before becoming the Nationals, the team started as the Montreal Expos in 1969. As Canada's first MLB team, the Expos brought big-league baseball north of the border. In the team's first season, pitcher Bill Stoneman threw a **no-hitter**, claiming one of the first great moments in team history!

26

The Expos started shipping big wins in the late 1970s and early 1980s. From 1979 to 1983, the team had five winning seasons. By 1981, Montreal made the playoffs for the first time and reached the **National League** (**NL**) Championship Series.

18
expos

GAMETIME

In 2005, the team moved to Washington, DC, and became the Nationals. In their first season, the team finished with an 81–81 **record**. Slugger Nick Johnson hit 15 home runs and earned 74 **RBIs**, helping the Nats get off to a strong start in their new home.

GRAND SLAMS

The Nationals built a powerful roster with top draft picks like Ryan Zimmerman and Bryce Harper. In 2012, the Nationals won 98 games, the most in team history. They also won the **NL** East! Pitcher Gio González finished the regular season with a major-league-best 21 wins.

ZIMMERMANN
27

In 2014, the Nationals had the best **ERA** in the league. Jordan Zimmermann led the way with 14 wins and a **no-hitter** in the last game of the regular season. The team finished with 96 wins and won the **NL** East. In the playoffs, the Nationals faced the Giants in an 18-inning game. It was the longest match in MLB **postseason** history!

2019 WORLD CHAMPIONS
FIGHT FINISHED
THANK YOU, NATIONALS FANS!
DELTA
WASHINGTON NATIONALS
BIG BUS
AK86
2019 WORLD CHAMPIONS
DELTA

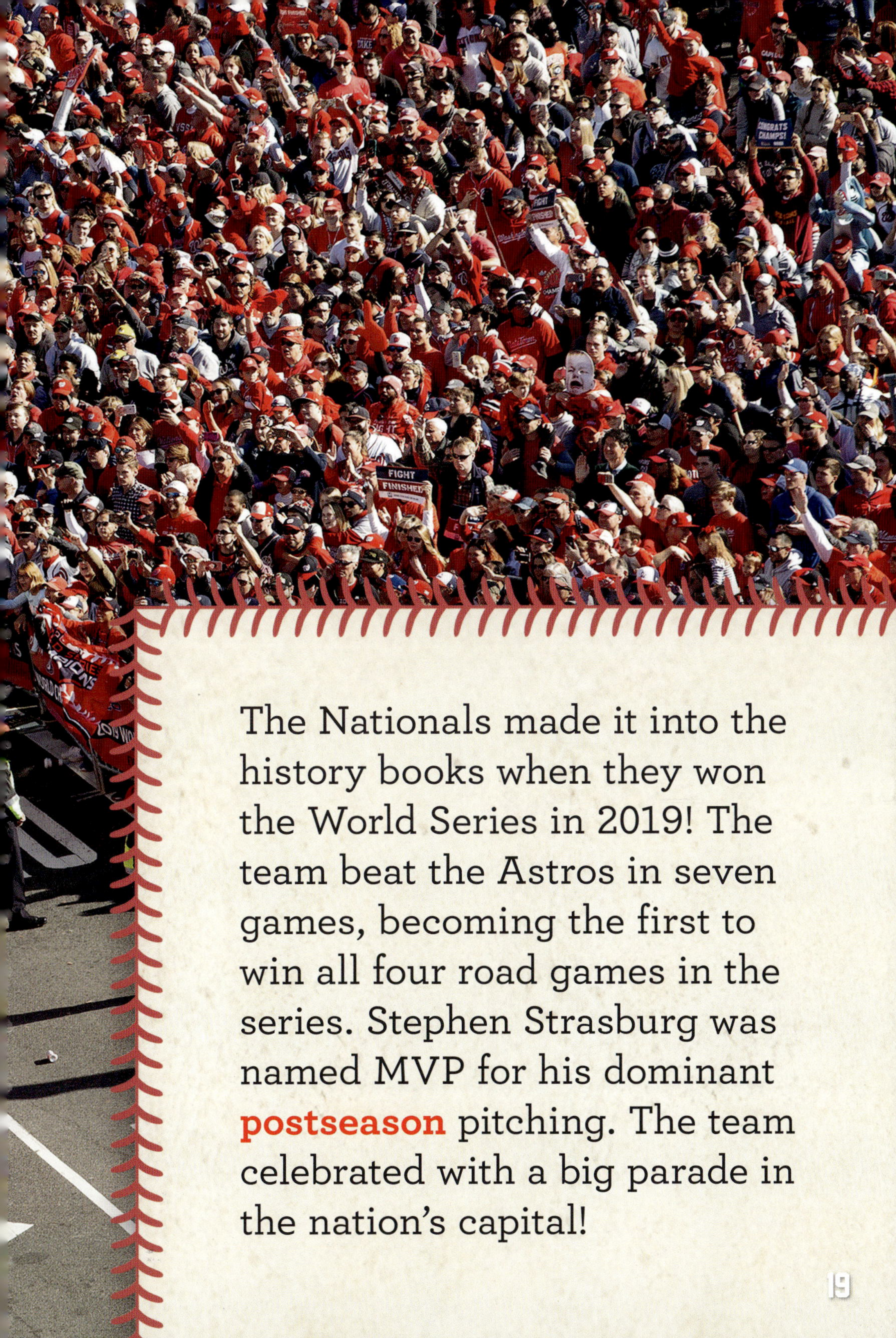

The Nationals made it into the history books when they won the World Series in 2019! The team beat the Astros in seven games, becoming the first to win all four road games in the series. Stephen Strasburg was named MVP for his dominant **postseason** pitching. The team celebrated with a big parade in the nation's capital!

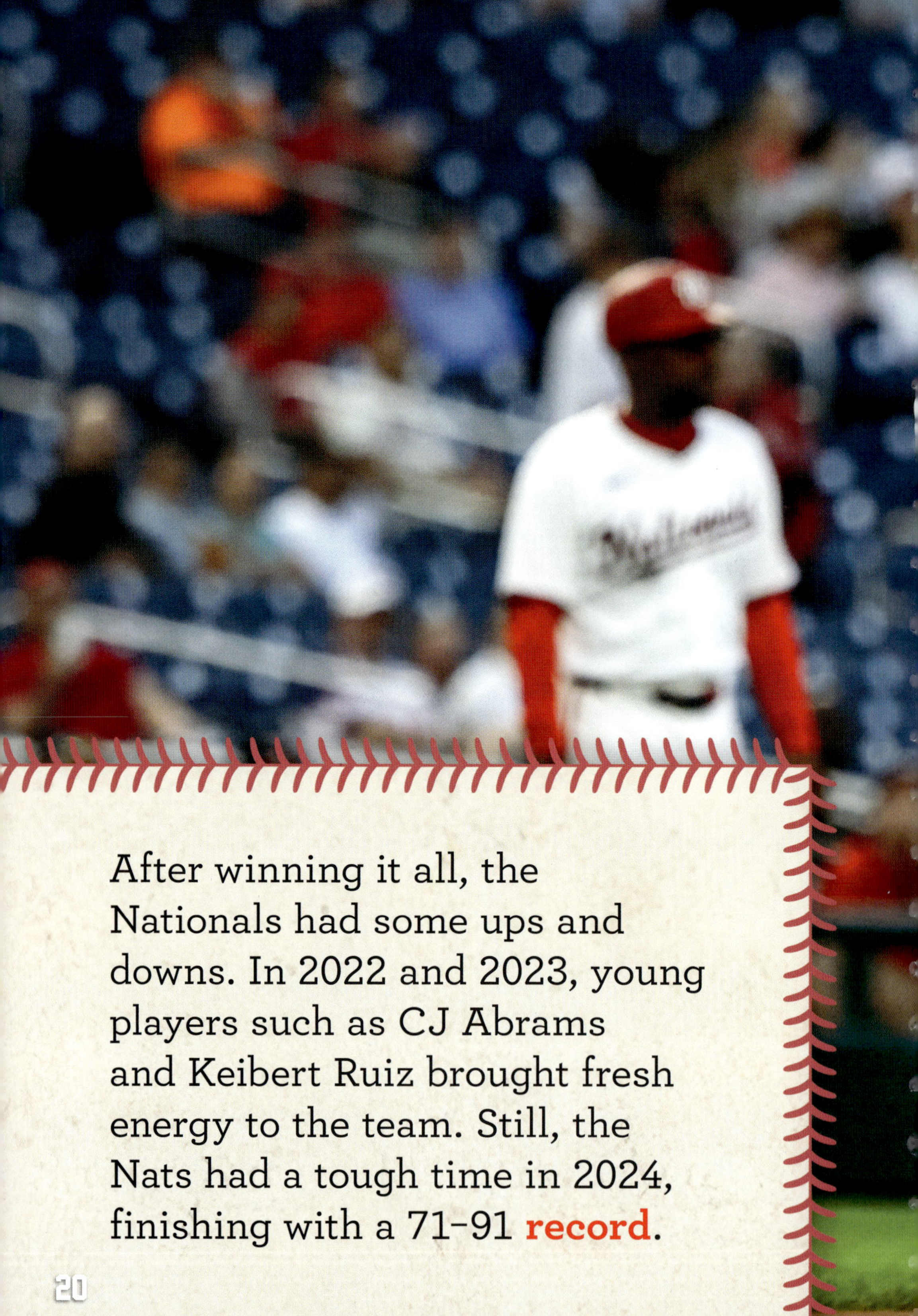

After winning it all, the Nationals had some ups and downs. In 2022 and 2023, young players such as CJ Abrams and Keibert Ruiz brought fresh energy to the team. Still, the Nats had a tough time in 2024, finishing with a 71–91 **record**.

Nationals
WASHINGTON NATIONALS
5

WASHINGTON NATIONALS
Rawlings

In 2025, the Nationals celebrated 20 seasons in Washington, DC. MacKenzie Gore made his first **All-Star** team and finished the season with 185 strikeouts and a 4.17 **ERA**. **Rookie** Robert Hassell III had a **walk-off** hit in his first game, giving fans a look at a baseball campaign that could win big!

HALL OF FAME

Gary Carter was not just a star catcher for the Expos—he could hit dingers too! Carter was a seven-time **All-Star** with Montreal and won three **Gold Gloves** as catcher. He also smashed more than 200 home runs with the Expos. Carter was named to the Baseball Hall of Fame in 2003.

Andre Dawson was a strong outfielder and a monster hitter for the Expos from 1976 to 1986. Dawson won **Rookie** of the Year in 1977 and went on to earn six **Gold Gloves** with Montreal. With 225 home runs hit for the Expos, he was named to the Baseball Hall of Fame in 2010.

From 1979 to 1990, Tim Raines was a lightning-fast outfielder and top-tier hitter for the Expos. He made seven **All-Star** teams and won a batting title in 1986. Raines stole 70 or more bases six times, with a high of 90 in 1983. He had 635 steals and over 1,200 hits for the team. Raines joined the Baseball Hall of Fame in 2017.

expos

GLOSSARY

All-Star – an athlete named to the yearly baseball contest where top players from the American League and the NL compete against each other, or the team consisting of All-Star athletes.

Earned-Run Average (ERA) – the average number of earned runs per game scored against a pitcher.

Gold Glove – an annual award given to the best fielders at each position in both the American League (AL) and NL.

National League (NL) – one of two 15-team leagues that make up MLB.

no-hitter – a game in which a pitcher doesn't allow any hits.

postseason – the playoffs, including the wild-card round, divisional playoffs, league championship series, and World Series.

record – a team's season total of wins and losses.

rookie – a professional athlete in his or her first season in a sport.

Runs Batted In (RBI) – a statistic that credits a batter for making a play that allows a run to be scored.

walk-off – any victory in which the home team scores the winning run in the bottom of the final inning.

ONLINE RESOURCES

To learn more about the Washington Nationals, please visit **abdobooklinks.com** or scan this QR code. These links are routinely monitored and updated to provide the most current information available.

INDEX